CW01652096

... THE

OLD GAOL

A HISTORY OF THE BUILDING

BY

KATE FEARN

THE ELY SOCIETY 2001

Published by The Ely Society 2001
© Kate Fearn. ISBN 0 903616 19 X

FRONT COVER *View of west elevation of gaol with the Octagon in the background* (photo: RCHME)

Introduction

In 1997, Ely museum moved from its former premises on High Street to the Old Gaol on the corner of Lynn Road and Market Street (front cover). This Grade II listed building is of stone and brick construction, double-pile in plan with a tiled, hipped roof. It is best known for housing the Bishop of Ely's gaol from c.1679 until 1836. A programme of documentary research and archaeological survey conducted by the author during the museum conversion revealed much evidence relating to the gaol period. Many of the finds are now on display in the museum and the story of the gaol is recounted in Gallery 7. However, its use as a gaol represents a relatively short episode in the history of the building, parts of which date back to the medieval period. This guide summarises the evidence for the medieval building, its subsequent development and use as the bishop's gaol and later phases of alteration to the present day.

PHASE 1
The 1417 building

The earliest documentary reference to a building on this site dates to 1417, when a detailed survey of the town was carried out to resolve a dispute over property ownership between the bishop and the prior. The rents of all properties along each road in the town are listed systematically and the tenement of Thomas Hakwrong, referred to as 'Aletnin', is recorded on the site of the Old Gaol. The modern layout of the town, well established by 1417, appears to have originated in the thirteenth century and it is possible that the earliest parts of the Old Gaol date back to this period. Indeed, the excavation of foundation trenches for the museum extension revealed an homogenous layer of brown sandy loam containing twelfth and thirteenth century potsherds, which corresponded with the earliest floor-level inside the building.

The south range of the Old Gaol incorporates medieval stonework (FIGURE 1). The fabric comprises unsorted medium-brown sandstone rubble and survives to its greatest extent in the west gable, where it can be traced to a height of 5.7m above present ground-level (FIGURE 2). The east and south walls were built in brick in the eighteenth century, masking the original stonework, which survives behind. Selective removal of plaster revealed Phase 1 fabric in the north wall at ground and first floor levels.

This was a substantial stone building, rectangular in plan, with internal measurements of 11.7m (east-west) by approximately 5.75m (north-south), and walls up to 0.9m thick. The proportions of the building are approximately 2:1, a ratio commonly found in great halls of the thirteenth and fourteenth centuries.

There is evidence for a window in the west gable, though all that survives of this is a jamb comprising six chamfered limestone blocks (FIGURE 2). The position of the jamb indicates that the window was placed centrally and quite high up in the gable. The stone jamb of a second window, which may date to this period, was found towards the east end of the north wall on removal of a fireplace. A shallow groove towards the top of the jamb may have held a shutter, secured by a bar housed in a socket visible in the centre of the jamb (c, FIGURE 1 – visible in Gallery ①).

The position of the window in the west gable suggests that this was probably a single storey building, possibly comprising an open hall heated by a central hearth, as shown in the reconstruction on display in Gallery ⑦. If the high table was located at the west end of the building, under the window, the main entrance is likely to have been towards the east end of the north or south walls. The existing doorway in the north wall (a, FIGURE 1, now in a cupboard) probably originated in this phase, though the brick-built door surround dates to the sixteenth century (phase 2).

The location of the building is of significance when considering its function, at a comfortable distance from the market on the corner of two major roads approaching the centre of town from the north and east. It was also one of the few properties referred to by name in the 1417 survey, factors which may be indicative of status. It is possible that it fulfilled some municipal function, perhaps associated with the market.

PHASE 2
The Fifteenth and Sixteenth Centuries

During the 1997 conversion of the building to house the museum, a brick doorway was revealed in the north wall of the hall range (b, FIGURE 1 – Gallery ④). It dates to the late-fifteenth–sixteenth century on stylistic grounds, having a four-centred head and moulded brick jambs and was originally plastered, presumably to resemble stone. The north side of the doorway is simply treated with an outline of single-chamfered bricks. The more elaborately moulded door-check is positioned on the south (hall) side of the opening, suggesting that the door gave access to a room beyond the hall, rather than opening to the exterior of the building. The door was blocked on the north side by the insertion of a chimney-stack in the seventeenth century. It is possible that this narrow doorway gave access to a projecting stair-turret, as three substantial principal joists running north-south across the hall bear mouldings dating to the sixteenth century, suggesting that a floor was inserted in the hall at this time. Alternatively, a more substantial north wing may have been built to provide additional living space as well as housing stairs to give access to the upper floor. Unfortunately, evidence for the form of the stair-turret or wing was destroyed or hidden by the construction of the present north range.

Heating for part of the building in this phase was provided by a lateral chimney-stack, inserted into the north wall of the hall to the west of the doorway (1, FIGURE 1, ground floor). Evidence for this was found on removal of a nineteenth century fireplace surround, which revealed the moulded brick jambs of a fireplace contemporary with the adjacent door. The chamfered brick jambs of a first-floor fireplace, served by the same stack, were uncovered in the room above (2, FIGURE 1, first floor).

PHASE 3
The Seventeenth Century

During this period, documentary evidence indicates that the building functioned as a private house and may have been a tavern. Structurally, the building was extended to the north by 5.50m with the addition of a new, two storied stone range (FIGURES 2 & 3). This was built up against the north wall of the phase 1 building, and extends along its whole length, creating a substantial stone building on the then popular double-pile plan.

The north and west walls of this range survive to a maximum height of 4.40m, rising to approximately 4.85m on the east elevation. Greensand rubble is the principal building material, though it differs from the Phase 1 masonry in that it is laid in horizontal courses of similar height, with thick mortar joints incorporating small lumps of Greensand, a technique comparable to galleting. A further distinctive feature is the incorporation of tile courses.

The junction between Phases 1 and 3 is marked by a straight-joint on the west and east elevations and by reduction in the height of the plinth which runs around the west and north elevations. Original windows from this phase have been replaced by later openings. Access to this range from the exterior was through a doorway in the north wall, positioned in line with the entrance to the Phase 1 range and linked to it by a passage.

The inside of the building was extensively remodelled during this period. The existing lateral chimney stack was considerably enlarged, with additional flues added to the east, blocking doorway 'b' and providing heating for G3 and F6. A new lateral stack was constructed further to the east in the centre wall (5, FIGURE 1) and fireplaces were opened in G4 (blocking window 'c') and in F1. Access between the floors was gained from a staircase constructed in the angle between the main stack and the north wall of the Phase 1 building.

The dimensions of the north range and the position of the main floor joists suggest that it was divided into three rooms on each floor. The main beams supporting the first-floor are original and those visible in G3 and the passage have curved and stepped chamfer stops. This decorative device also occurs on the wooden lintels spanning the fireplaces in F1 and F6. Such chamfer stops have been recorded in buildings dating from the sixteenth to the eighteenth centuries, with a large number of seventeenth century examples. Comparable chamfer stops occur on a fireplace lintel in the Queen's Hall, Ely, which was inserted after 1649. The plastered brick jambs of the fireplace in F6 are also chamfered, with plain curved stops.

The Bishop's Gaol – c.1679-1764

The bishops of Ely, as lords of the Liberty, were responsible for all administrative duties normally carried out by sheriffs or by royal commissioners. The bishop held the right to arrest, sentence and imprison throughout the Liberty of Ely, which included sizeable areas of Norfolk and Suffolk as well as the Isle itself. The bishop is known to have had gaols in Ely, Wisbech and Donnington in Suffolk.

The building now known as the Old Gaol did not function as a gaol until 1679 at the earliest, as in this year, it is listed in the Ely Porta Manorial Survey and Rental as a tenement occupied by John Austin and Will Kibble. However, it is likely that the change of use took place soon after this, as the entry is crossed out, and the words 'Ely Barton', synonymous with the bishop's gaol, written alongside. The building was certainly functioning as a gaol before the death of Bishop Gunning in 1686. However, it soon became ruinous and as Bishop Mawson refused to repair it, the gaoler was forced to secure convicted felons with heavy irons. The bishop claimed he knew nothing of the conditions suffered in the gaol and continued to deny all responsibility for the maintenance of the building. An enquiry into the conditions at the gaol began in 1764 and found that repairs had been paid for in the past by Bishops Gunning, Cox and Heton, though at other times, the county had paid. For example, a Quarter Session meeting in 1714 made a rate for the repair of the gaol. Some inhabitants refused to pay this and were subsequently imprisoned in the gaol. Repairs carried out in 1725 were funded by voluntary contributions amounting to about £170. The Grand Jury at the Assizes in 1729 presented the gaol as out of repair once more, but little was done. In 1759, the gaol was reported as almost ruinous but was still not repaired.

The conversion of what was a private house into the Bishop's gaol would appear to have been achieved with minimal alteration and cost. The accommodation for the prisoners was probably located in the newer, and presumably more secure, north range. This is implied by the existence of small cell windows into the north wall. There were three windows on the ground-floor and two on the first-floor (FIGURE 3). The sash window at the east-end of this wall and that in the west gable end may have replaced smaller cell windows, as is suggested in the reconstruction on display in Gallery ⑦.

On visiting the prison in 1764, Mr James Collyer, a magistrate, was appalled by what he saw and immediately sent a petition to Bishop Mawson, demanding that something be done about 'the cruelties exercised towards the prisoners in Ely gaol.' When the bishop failed to reply, a letter, accompanied with an illustration of the methods used to secure the prisoners, was sent to the King (FIGURE 4). The petition was finally heard before the Privy Council sitting at Whitehall on 25 March, 1765. The gaoler at that time was William Armiger and he described the condition of the gaol:

> 'It is an old house turned into a gaol, the inward wall is plaister, the outward wall is so bad that any man may break through. The debtors and felons can hold conference together. The petition [partition] is so thin – a convict broke out with his Irons on, weighing 60 pounds since the gaol was repaired.'

The Privy Council Committee heard that the use of irons to secure prisoners as illustrated in the sketch was first implemented when:

> 'about seven years ago, several men and women being charged with diverse robberies in Whittlessea were committed to Ely gaol, and as they belonged to one gang and were very hardened and desperate, there was great reason to apprehend that an escape would be attempted...'

After the escape and recapture of one of the men, the gaoler fixed a spiked iron collar around his neck and was obliged to 'shinbolt him and lock him down' in order to secure him in the ruinous building. After this experience, one of the cells was converted into a strong room, where prisoners were secured:

> 'There is a large Bar and Shackles, and six men chained down as described by the drawing ... Deponent [Armiger] has been obliged to buy Irons for his security against a Felon who had been guilty of breaking into some of his Outhouses. The Debtors are not ironed unless they are outrageous, they are obliged to be kept among the Desperate Felons who are always contriving to break out. The Gaoler secure 'em in a strong manner as he can and is oblig'd to keep persons to watch'.

It was claimed during the hearing that Bishop Mawson made £500 clear profit a year from his jurisdiction and should therefore pay for the upkeep of the gaol. This 'shameful assertion' was strongly denied by the bishop. The report on the Committee concluded that:

> 'the house used for a Gaol is very improper for that purpose, in respect to its structure, of its having no convenient accommodation for the separate Confinement of Criminals and Debtors, and its present weakness and ruinous Condition, the state of which, renders it impossible to secure prisoners who are disposed to escape but by the means of Irons, which are increas'd in weight and in various modes of pressure in proportion to the danger of their escaping, or being rescued.'

It was decided that if the bishop did not agree to repair the gaol, the matter would be settled at the Court of the King's Bench. However, rather than continue the contention further, Bishop Mawson submitted and agreed to repair the gaol. A plan and estimate (now lost) was prepared in 1767 and work commenced almost immediately, and was completed after seven months at a cost of about £500, which matches the annual sum thought to have been earned by the Bishop from his jurisdiction. This was a sizeable sum of money in the eighteenth century and the restoration work must have been substantial. It constitutes the fourth phase in the structural alteration of the Old Gaol.

PHASE 4
The Bishop's Gaol – 1767 repairs

Examination of the fabric shows that the repair of the building in 1767 was largely confined to the south range, the oldest part. The south wall of the gaol was rebuilt in brick, on a slightly different alignment as the original stone wall but incorporating parts of its fabric. This wall is of one build and is constructed in Flemish bond using yellow bricks of standard size. The four, flat arched windows in the south facade do not open and comprise rectangular quarries of glass held in lead cames braced by saddle bars. They are barred on the inside and sloping boards or louvres were originally fitted to the exterior to prevent prisoners looking out.

The south wall terminates with a brick shaft, of the same build, which projects into the gaol yard. This housed the two indoor privies, one located in the south-east corner of F1 and originally ventilated by a small window, and the other above in G1. Waste from the privies and the gutters discharged into a brick vaulted chamber below the gaol yard. A drinking trough, accessible from the exercise yard, was built into the projection. The east wall of the south range is keyed into the privy block and the Flemish bond is contemporary with it, though the colour of the bricks used is more variable. On the ground-floor level, there is a window identical in style to those in the south elevation. To the north of this window, a doorway, blocked on the exterior but visible as a recess on the interior gave access to the exercise yard. The fabric of the Phase 1 building lies behind the brick facade on this elevation. The ground floor window in the west wall of the south range is attributed to the rebuilding of 1767 on stylistic grounds, being closely comparable to those already described in the south and east walls.

Probably at the same time, the three walls of the north range built, during Phase 3, were raised in brick up to the eaves level of the south range. The English bond brickwork is similar to that surrounding the ground floor window in the west elevation, which also dates to 1767. A double hipped and tiled roof was erected over the consolidated ranges. This roof survives largely intact, though some of the pine timbers were replaced in 1991. The fenestration of the north range appears to have been altered by blocking some of the small cell windows in use in Phase 3 and replacing others by the insertion of larger openings, as the prisoners' accommodation became more concentrated in the rebuilt south range.

Descriptions of the Gaol by Howard and Neild

Towards the end of the eighteenth century, John Howard travelled throughout Britain exposing abuses and scandals in the prison system. His important work, State of the Prisons in England and Wales (1777) provided the impetus for improvements in the design and management of prisons. He visited Ely Gaol in 1774 and 1776, recording useful information about the facilities in the gaol, its layout and management. He also described conditions in the Bridewell, which was at that time located in a thatched building adjacent to the gaol, fronting Market Street.

Until the late-eighteenth century, when salaries were first introduced at Ely, the gaoler made his living from the fees collected on the arrival of prisoners (15s. 3d. for debtors and 13s. 4d. for felons) and by providing them with various goods and services. For example, a charge of £5 was made for the transportation of prisoners from the gaol to the sea-ports and then on to Australia, a practice which began after Captain Cook annexed New South Wales for Britain in 1770. Prisoners largely relied upon the support of their family, friends and the proceeds of the begging box for food and drink. Another source of income was the *garnish*, a fee payable by new prisoners to be shared amongst those already inside to pay for beer. When Howard visited Ely, this was set at 1s 4d. The gaoler encouraged this practise as he kept the proceeds from 'the tap'. Those unfortunates who could not pay were stripped of their clothes and any belongings. Howard proposed the abolition of the garnish and by 1802 it was apparently obsolete at Ely.

In most prisons, men, women, debtors and felons were kept apart, though before the repair of the bishop's gaol in 1767, debtors shared cells with felons, at least for part of the day. After 1767, there were two grades of accommodation in the gaol: the cheap and basic 'common-side' cells and the superior 'master's side' cells. Many of the men and women imprisoned at Ely were debtors, as was the case in most of gaols in England and Wales at this time. They were confined until their debts, including those accrued from the purchase of a bed and other comforts inside the gaol, had been paid, usually by family or friends.

Howard notes that there were three 'master's side' cells upstairs for the debtors imprisoned at Ely. The cell for condemned felons was also located on this floor. On the ground-floor, there was the Felons' day-room (also referred to as the Felons' Hall) and their night-cell, with a window 'about a foot square.' There was no straw and no infirmary. The debtors and felons each had their own courtyard. The felons' yard was polluted by a sewer and had no water supply. The debtors had use of a court-yard with pump, which also served as the gaoler's garden, to the north of the building. Howard was clearly unimpressed by what he saw and despite his recommendations, he returned on December 4, 1787, to find that little had been done to improve conditions:

> 'No alterations. The felons' court not secure; but water being now laid on, I am persuaded, from the humanity of the bishop, they will have use of it. Allowance now 1lb. of bread. Neither clauses against spirituous liqueur, nor the act for preserving the health of prisoners hung up. The gaol not whitewashed for three years. Transports have not the two shillings and sixpence a week. The iron bars and ring still remain in the room in which criminals were, formerly, cruelly confined. Gaoler's salary only £10.'

John Neild continued the work begun by Howard, paying three visits to the gaol in 1801, 1802 and 1805. On his visit in 1805, he found conditions much improved, praising those responsible for providing 'better ventilation, county-clothing, and bath; for the regular entry of their visits in a book, and for the great cleanliness and good order in which every part is kept.' A 'nursery room' on the first-floor was set apart for the sick and a surgeon attended the gaol when required. The most unfortunate prisoners slept on straw provided by the county, though the gaoler supplemented his salary by providing bedding at various rates. Neild records 'One iron bedstead (made a present of to the Gaol by the Bishop's Lady), and one wooden bedstead for the Nursery. The keeper furnishes beds at 1s, 1s 6d and 2s per week, according to the circumstances of the prisoner.' The

PLATE 1 *Plank partition in the felon's day room* (RCHME)

windows were glazed and were fitted with 'sloping boards before the iron gratings to prevent prisoners looking into the street.'

Neild records that the condemned cell on the first-floor measured 15' 6" by 13' 6" and was 8' 10" high. It was ventilated by an iron grated window and an aperture in the door about 6" square. Neild describes the scene within: 'Across the floor are 26 iron bars and staples fixed in the floor, to which prisoners are fastened by a strong iron chain run through the main link of their fetters, and, passing through the side of the door, is locked on the outside.' Despite the enquiry of 1765 and the subsequent rebuilding, condemned felons continued to be restrained as described by Nield:

> 'The irons used here are 18 or 19 pounds weight, and one pair 43 pounds, which, in 1799, one John Gothard, a transport, had on for 3 days; but, as his body swelled greatly in consequence, they were (on the surgeon's representation) taken off. There is only one iron collar with spikes now left; and the last time it was used was on James Thompson, in the year 1798.'

However, the conditions continued to improve for the majority of the prisoners. The felons' yard was supplied with water, an allowance of 5lb of wheat bread was dispensed every other day and religious services were performed once a week. By 1810, wooden beds with straw mattresses were provided in each sleeping room. More orderly and humane management of the gaol was also indicated by the display of the act for preserving the health of prisoners, the clauses against spirituous liquer and the rules and orders of the prison.

The Layout of the Gaol – 1767–1836

The function of certain rooms during the period 1767-1836 can be surmised using the structural and documentary evidence, the descriptions of the gaol by Howard and Neild and the tradesmens' bills contained in the bailiff's accounts.

The Felons' Hall *(FIGURE 1 G1)*

When the building was restored in 1767, the ground-floor of the south range was used to accommodate the prisoners during the day. Any existing cross-walls were removed, and a massive oak partition inserted (perhaps on the line of an earlier partition) to divide G1 into two day rooms (plate 1, Galleries ④ and ⑤). Removal of lath and plaster from the east face of the partition revealed the massive oak planks laid horizontally, edge-to-edge, to give maximum strength. Carpenter's marks scribed across the joins indicate that the planks were cut in the workshop and assembled on site. The planks are nailed to vertical posts tenoned at intervals into a sill beam. The use of horizontal edge-to-edge planking such as this is unusual in ordinary domestic contexts, with known examples being largely confined to prisons and strong rooms, where strength was a functional requirement, for example, in the Court house, Milton Regis, Kent and the gaol at Appleby, Cumbria. By 1814, the joints between the oak planks in the partition had 'shrunk from each other near an inch.' In order 'to prevent hiding places of instruments or anything to effect escape or doing mischief' the gaps between the joints were covered with strips of iron. This 'hooping' was removed when the partition was plastered, but its position is marked by traces of rust and nail holes along the edge of each plank. There are traces of white-wash or gesso on the planks and numerous scratches, though no certain examples of graffiti.

The room to the east of the partition is referred to as the felons' hall in the tradesmens' bills. It gave direct access to the exercise yard via a doorway in the north end of the east wall. It was heated by a fireplace in the south wall, which had to be enlarged in 1793, as 'there were scarce passage or draft for the smoak, and so constructed as not to admit of sweeping, by which many people were almost suffocated.' The quoins forming the splay to the former window in the north wall of the felons' hall (c, FIGURE 1) are engraved with graffiti including the names of prisoners. The room on the west side of the partition was used as a day room for prisoners until the early nineteenth century, when pine panelling was added to the south wall. The earliest date for the panelling is provided by a piece of 1804 newspaper attached to the back. The muntins, stiles and rails are moulded and there is evidence to suggest that the design incorporated a carved frieze. The insertion of this decorative panelling suggests a considerable elevation in the status of the room. It is possible that it was converted into a parlour for the use of the gaoler.

The felons' night cell *(FIGURE 1 G2)*

The felons' cell or night room was on the ground-floor. Nield records that it measured approximately 5.50m by 3.05m and was lit by a window about

PLATE 2 *First-floor cell layout prior to museum conversion* (RCHME)

0.30m square. The dimensions of G2 best fit this description. Moreover, this room was also lit by a small barred window in the north wall (removed in Phase 6).

First-floor

Several reinforced cell doors dating to this phase remained in their original position until the 1997 conversion, including those to F1, F2 (former debtors' cells) and F7 (the condemned cell; Plate 2). Built for strength, the doors to F1 and F2 comprise a double skin of horizontally laid planks, with vertical planks making up the door to F7. All three doors retain their original bolts and hinges and each incorporates a small and heavily barred window through which the gaoler could view the prisoners. The doors to F3 and F6 are of similar construction though they have no window.

The Debtors' Cells (FIGURE 1 F1–F4)

Three of the four rooms in the south range (F1–F4) were 'good-sized' debtors cells. Removal of the lath and plaster from the west partition in F1 and the north wall of F2 revealed pine planks, approximately 0.20m high and 0.02m deep, nailed edge-to-edge, horizontally, to vertical posts set at intervals in the floor and ceiling joists. Iron strips were nailed over vulnerable parts of the planking, such as the vertical joins between the planks and around the doors. The top edge of each plank has a beading similar to that found on skirting boards of the period and it seems highly likely that they were originally made as such.

The planks revealed in F1 and F2 are covered in graffiti, including names, monograms, dates and several sketches of gallows. Most of the graffiti is scratched or carved into the soft-wood, with occasional use of lead and ink. (Plate 4).

For added security, the ceilings in cells F1 and F3 are boarded. The joints between the boards, which are laid edge-to-edge, are sealed with long strips of pine. The original grated windows survive in F2 and F3. Cell F1 was unique in housing a privy, which is boxed in the south-east corner of the room. The ceiling of the former privy is reinforced with iron strips similar to those securing the plank partitions. These may have been added in 1783-1784, when W. Cullen was paid for 4' of iron and four iron bars for the privy, perhaps after an escape attempt.

PLATE 3 *Interior of condemned cell* (AUTHOR)

The Condemned Cell *(FIGURE 1, F7)*
F7 has been identified as the condemned cell on the basis of documentary and structural evidence. A bathroom was installed in the south end of the former cell some time during Phase 5, though the reinforced cell door was retained in its original position. During the conversion into the museum, the toilet with associated partition was removed and the surviving section of the original west partition revealed to the south of the cell door (plate 3). The inside face of the partition was lined with horizontally laid pine planks, reinforced with iron strips nailed to the wood at vertical intervals. The original pine floorboards, with indents marking the former position of the iron bars, were revealed below the modern floorboards. Neild records that the prisoners were fastened to these bars by 'a strong iron chain run through the main link of their fetters' (shackles for the feet), which passed 'through the side of the door' and was locked on the outside in the passage. The square hole through which this chain passed survives and is reinforced with iron strips. This woodwork was recorded *in situ* in advance of its removal to the west end of the south wall in 1997 (Gallery ⑦). Fragments of a contemporary wooden spoon with a broad handle incised with tally marks were found on removal of the planking. The door to the condemned cell, comprising a double skin of vertical planks reinforced with iron straps, was moved to the top of the new staircase in 1997. The early-nineteenth century sash window in the north wall is likely to have replaced the original iron-grated window recorded by Howard and Nield.

Removal of the wall-paper covering a chimney flu projecting from the south wall of the former condemned cell revealed drawings of a 'fleet' of at least five sailing ships extending across the wall. Although the mural is extremely faint and completely worn away or obscured by plaster in places, it is still possible to see ships in full sail, equipped with tiers of gun-ports and rigging. Similar ships were used to transport convicts to the colonies throughout the eighteenth and nineteenth centuries and it is possible that the artist had been sentenced to such a trip. Adjacent to the mural is a faint inscription carved into the plaster, covering an area of about 1.00m by 0.60m. Each letter is 0.08m high and is carefully carved in uppercase Latin script, which reads:

PLATE 4 *Detail of graffiti in first-floor cell* (RCHME)

PRAY GOD
GOOD PEOPLE
RE MEMBER THE
POOR PRISONERS

The condemned cell was supposedly the most secure room in the gaol, and judging by the methods used to secure prisoners, it is not surprising that the tradesmens' bills contain many references to repairs and reinforcements to the floor, ceiling, walls and iron-work. For example, in 1796, Thomas Winter, carpenter, was paid £16 7s 6d for 'repairing ye breaches and where ye Prisoners broke Prison.' This included repairing the floor and fitting a new door-frame and shutters. In the same year, Jonathon Talbot, bricklayer, cut a ' 48' run of chaceing grooves in walls to receive end of boards to ceiling.' William Cullen's work in 1799 included fitting 69' of iron hooping, adding three strong links to the chain and fixing them to the floor with three large staples.

The Lodge

There are several references in the bailiff's accounts to a building in the yard known as the 'Lodge'. In 1793, Henry Rickwood, bricklayer, was paid for 'Strength'ning, tyeing up and proping up' the 'old building in the yard.' Thomas Winter, carpenter, also worked 'At the old lodge in the yard which was in danger of falling in.' In the same year, the main gaol building was insured for £450 with the Sun Fire Office. The Lodge, insured on the same policy for £50, is described as 'Brick & Tyled'. In 1814, Jonathon Talbot, bricklayer, received payment for tiling the 'lodge next to the turnpike', which suggests that it was located on the north side of the gaol building, adjacent to Lynn Road. A small building is shown in this position on the 1885 OS 1:500 map extract.

PHASE 5
1836-1995

The Inspector of Prisons, visiting Ely gaol in 1836, reported that it was 'most inefficient', describing the gaoler, Benjamin Barlow, as 'old, respectable and now physically incompetent' after thirty-four years of service. In the same year, an Act was passed which extinguished the secular jurisdiction of the archbishop of York and the bishop of Ely in certain liberties, thus abolishing the Liberty of Ely. Following this Act, the bishop's gaol at Ely was abolished. From then on, prisoners were committed to Cambridge County prison and the Old Gaol became a private house.

In 1842, the Ely Mechanics' Institute was established and its meetings and library were housed in the Old Gaol, by now the residence of Mr

Marshall Fisher, who became the Institute's librarian. The aim of the Institute was to instruct its members in 'every department of useful knowledge, party politics and controversy being rigidly excluded.'

From 1849, Mr Fisher and Mr Bard kept a museum in the building. Mr Fisher was an amateur scientist and enthusiastic collector of artifacts and natural history specimens. He curated the museum collections until his death at the age of 92 in 1899.

In 1904, many of the diocesan records were transferred to the Old Gaol from Bishop Alcock's tower in the Bishop's Palace. The custodian moved into the living quarters and a reading room was provided, with a store on the first-floor. The records remained there until c.1962, when they were moved to their present location in Cambridge University Library.

The administrative headquarters of East Cambridgeshire District Council was located in the building from October 1973 to March 1974. By July 1974, the City of Ely Council Chamber and office was on the first-floor and the old cells were used as storage by E.C.D.C. The ground-floor was occupied by the offices of the Registrar for births, deaths and marriages. The building was vacated in 1995 and plans drawn up for its conversion into Ely Museum.

PHASE 6
1996–1997

The re-location of Ely Museum from its High Street premises to the Old Gaol resulted in a major remodelling of the interior of the building between October 1996 and March 1997. The major part of this work was carried out by SS Ambrose of Ely, Ltd. The most significant changes to the building are summarised here:

G1 Complete removal of the oak partition. Most of the oak planking was re-used by attaching it to the eastside of a new partition inserted further to the east. This is now visible in Gallery 1 of the museum.

Doorway a, FIGURE 1: blocked.

Doorway b, FIGURE 1: revealed and consolidated in Gallery ②.

Fireplace 1, FIGURE 1: concealed.

G2 – Removal of old staircase and insertion of new, wider staircase in its place, with stair-lift for disabled access.

Former cell window in north wall blocked.

G3 – Fireplace 3, FIGURE 1: exposed.

Blocked cell window to east of casement revealed.

Partition between G3 and passage removed.

G4 – Phase 3 wall between G4 and passage removed.

Fireplace 5, FIGURE 1: removed to make doorway into G1.

Part of east wall removed for new access.

Staircase leading from passage retained but rendered inaccessible.

F1 – Fireplace 6, FIGURE 1: concealed.

Pine planking removed from west wall (south side) and re-erected on west wall of F3. New door cut through south side of west wall.

F2 – Cell door moved west of its original position in the north wall.

F3 – Converted into a reconstruction of the 'condemned cell': planking from west wall of F1 re-used on west wall. Barred 'viewing window' cut through partition between F3 and F4.

F4 – Fireplace 2, FIGURE 1: removed, flue sealed and new doorway inserted, giving access to F5.

F5 – West side converted into a reconstruction of a 'debtor's cell': insertion of partition and barred 'viewing window' in place of existing east partition.

F5-F6 – New staircase inserted on north side; west and centre windows in north wall blocked.

F6 – Fireplace 4, FIGURE 1: exposed.

F7 – Condemned cell door and surviving section of planking removed, complete with 'chain slot', from the west wall to the south wall. Cell door relocated to top of new staircase.

Construction of single storey north-west extension to the gaol building.

Construction of entrance porch on east side (north bay).

Architectural terms used

Brickwork:

- **English bond:** a method of laying bricks so that alternate courses on the face of the wall are composed of headers (ends) or stretchers (sides)
- **Flemish bond:** a method of laying bricks so that alternate headers (ends) and stretchers (sides) appear in each course on the face of the wall

Fenestration: the arrangement of windows in a wall

Flat arched window: window opening with a horizontal soffi (underside of the arch)

Gable: the head of wall at the end of a pitched roof, usually triangular but sometimes decoratively shaped

Galleting: technique of setting small pebbles or stone chips in a mortar course

Gesso: Gypsum based paint

Hipped roof: a roof with sloped ends instead of gables

Jamb: the side of an archway, doorway, window or other opening

Lath and plaster (wattle and daub): a method of wall construction consisting of branches or thin laths (wattles) roughly plastered over with mud or clay (daub)

Panelling: – Muntin: intermediate vertical post

- Rail: horizontal piece of frame
- Stile: vertical piece of frame

Quarry: in windows, a small pane of glass, generally square or diamond shaped

Saddlebar: a horizontal iron bar to which the glazing is secured

Sill beam: the lower horizontal beam into which vertical studs are tenon jointed

Stepped chamfer stop: a decorated block terminating a chamfered (or bevelled) moulding in stone or wood

Further Reading

Blakeman, P. 1990. *The Book of Ely*

Blakeman, P. 2001. *Ely Prisons*

Evans, R. 1982. *The Fabrication of Virtue: English Prison Architecture, 1750-1840*

Howard, J. 1777. *State of the Prisons in England and Wales*

Neild, J. 1808. *An Account of the Rise, Progress and Present State of the Society for the Discharge and Relief of Persons Imprisoned for Small Debts throughout England and Wales*

Victoria County Histories, Cambridgeshire, vols 2 and 4

Unpublished:

Minutes of the Privy Council, 1765, Cambridge University Library, Ely Diocesan Records

Acknowledgements

I would like to thank Anne Holton-Krayenbuhl and Philip Dixon for their help and advice during the survey and for sharing their thoughts on the phasing of the building. I am grateful to Pamela Blakeman and Mike Young for providing information relating to the gaol and for their useful comments on the text. Thanks are also due to Stephen Cole (RCHME) for his photographs of the building.

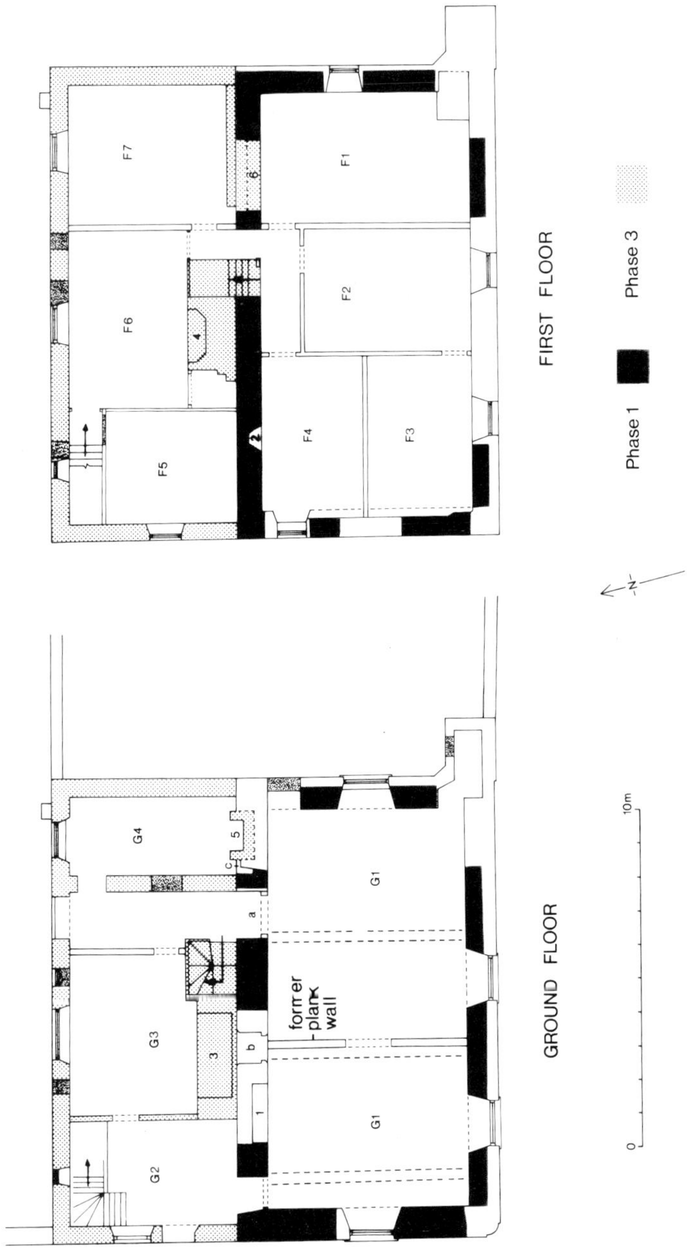

FIGURE 1 *Phased plans at ground (G) and first-floor (F) levels prior to museum conversion.*

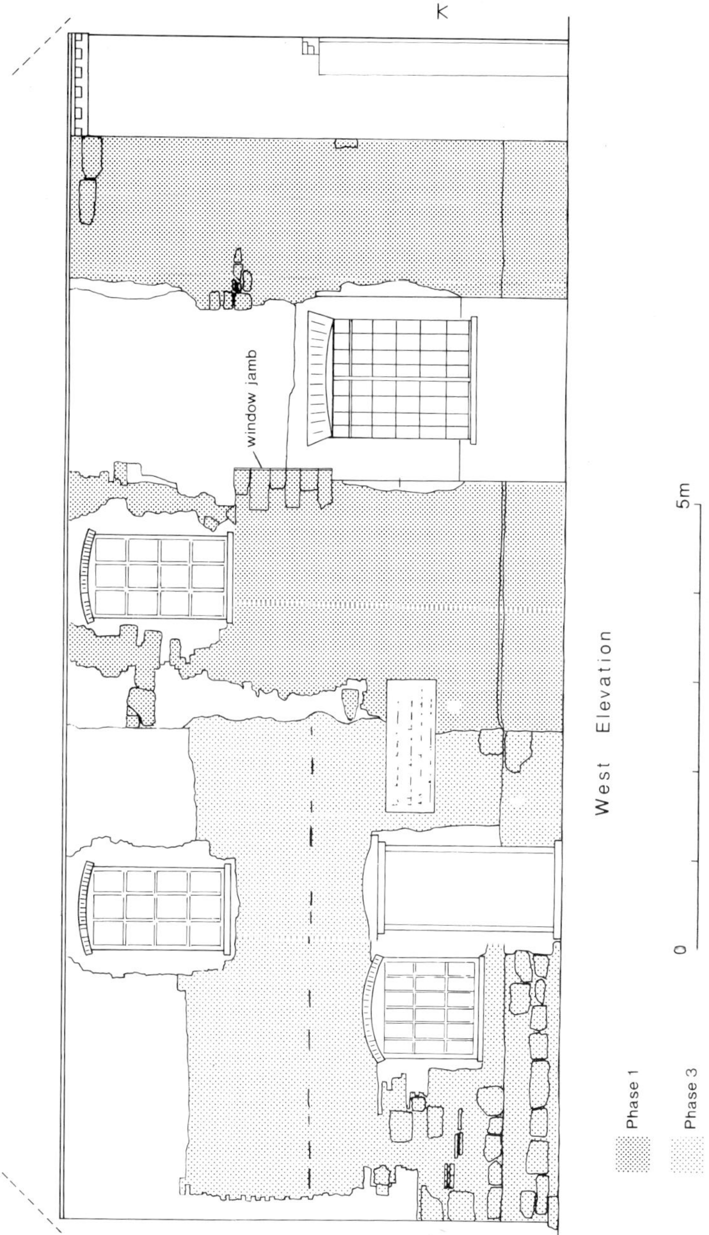

FIGURE 2 *West elevation, exterior*

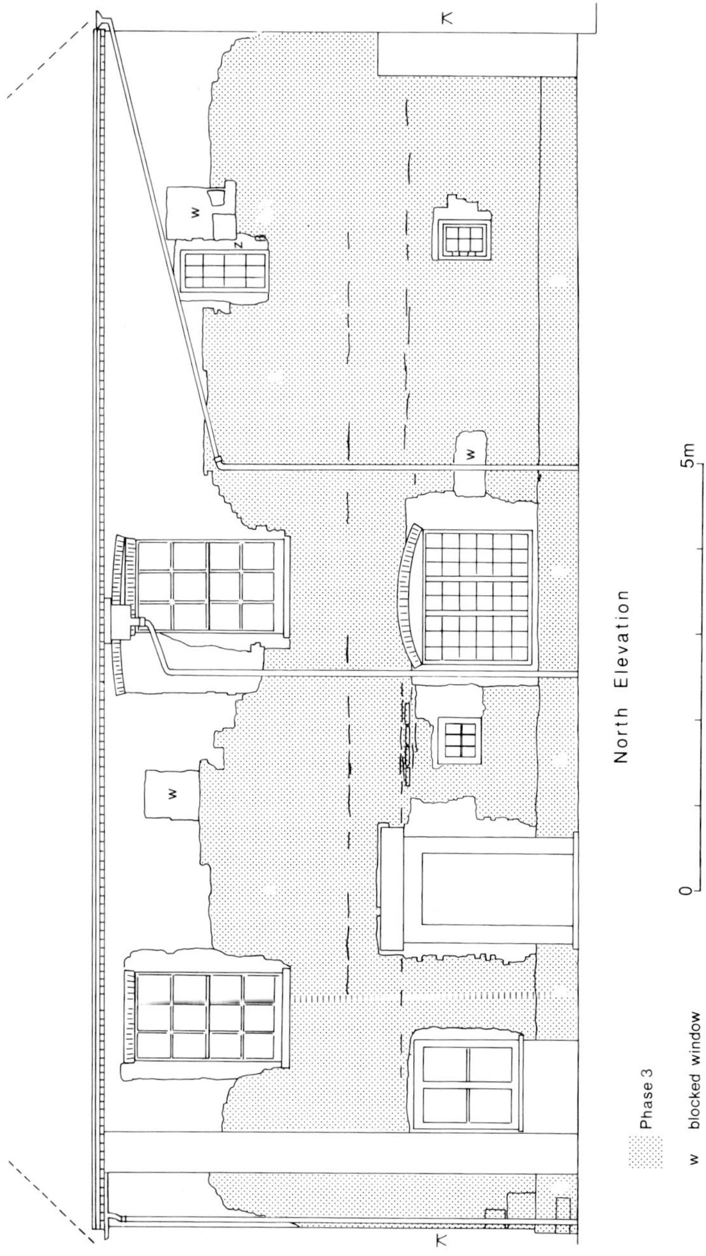

FIGURE 3 *North elevation, exterior*

TORTURE INFLICTED IN ELY PRISON IN 1768

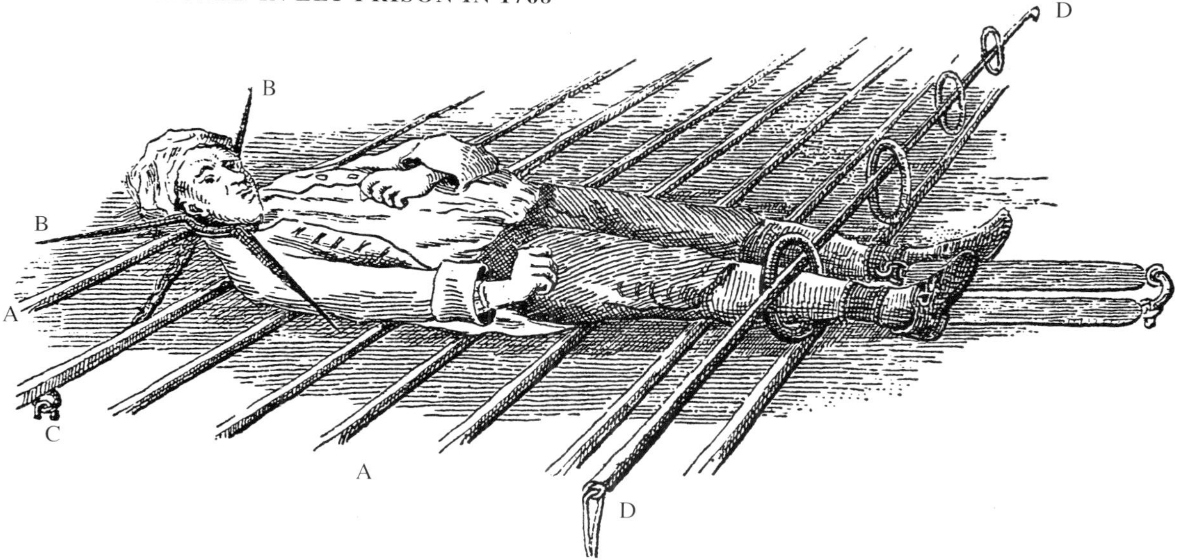

a a. – Iron bars, nailed to floor, which entered the flesh; **b** b. – Spikes 12 inches long fixed to a collar of iron $7\frac{1}{2}$ lbs. in weight, preventing a prisoner from resting his head on the ground; **c** c. – Chain which fasted the prisoner to the ground; **d** d. – Heavy iron bar crossing his legs and fastened to one, so preventing him changing his posture.

FIGURE 4 *Copy of a drawing made in c.1764 to illustrate the notorious use of irons in the condemned cell*